Get Upp!

Understanding Positive Psychology

Theresa Bodnar

Copyright © 2017 Theresa Bodnar.

All rights reserved. No part of this book may be used or reproduced by any means, graphic, electronic, or mechanical, including photocopying, recording, taping or by any information storage retrieval system without the written permission of the author except in the case of brief quotations embodied in critical articles and reviews.

Balboa Press books may be ordered through booksellers or by contacting:

Balboa Press
A Division of Hay House
1663 Liberty Drive
Bloomington, IN 47403
www.balboapress.com
1 (877) 407-4847

Because of the dynamic nature of the Internet, any web addresses or links contained in this book may have changed since publication and may no longer be valid. The views expressed in this work are solely those of the author and do not necessarily reflect the views of the publisher, and the publisher hereby disclaims any responsibility for them.

Any people depicted in stock imagery provided by Thinkstock are models, and such images are being used for illustrative purposes only. Certain stock imagery © Thinkstock.

ISBN: 978-1-5043-7138-4 (sc)
ISBN: 978-1-5043-7139-1 (e)

Library of Congress Control Number: 2016920638

Print information available on the last page.

Balboa Press rev. date: 01/18/2017

FOREWORD

This collection of poetry is dedicated to the positive psychology concepts I learned throughout the Certificate in Applied Positive Psychology (CAPP) program offered through the Flourishing Center.

That course changed my life in so many ways. I finally understood how my brain was wired (negative default), how my beliefs/thoughts impacted my emotions and behaviors, and was given tools to help me take charge of my thoughts, cultivate positivity, and forge my own pathway to flourishing and happiness.

After each on-site or distance learning, I felt inspired to write poems to help me simplify and retain the information presented. I had never written poetry before, but for some reason that form of artistic expression erupted within me. This book is a living example of my experience of "flow" in relation to this field. Creative energy filled me at the most unexpected times…in the middle of the night, on an airplane ride, in a coffee shop, at work…I just couldn't stop writing. In those moments, I never felt more alive, more connected, and more authentic.

The poems correspond with topics under the PERMA-V model: Positivity, Engagement, Relationships, Meaning and Purpose, Achievement and Vitality. To flourish, it is important for you to consciously address all of these areas.

I wanted to share these important concepts I learned about in the program to inspire you to live a more flourishing, happy life. Through the application of this newfound knowledge, the practice of self-awareness, and the utilization of these tools consistently, I (and many others) have noticed a change in me, sometimes described as a "glow". It's not that I wasn't ever happy or experiencing connection and flow in my life before- it just wasn't occurring as often or as authentically. Not everyone who smiles is happy, it's easy to fake it, but don't you want to really feel it? If you find yourself moved by what you read in this book and want to learn more, please check out The Flourishing Center at http://theflourishingcenter.com.

Chapter 1
Introduction to Positive Psychology

What is positive psychology? That's what I was wondering when I started this journey. I had been introduced to the field through the Resilience Training I'd received in the Army, and wanted to know more. I'm a lifelong learner, so when I googled "positive psychology" and The Flourishing Center's Certificate in Applied Positive Psychology came up, with it's first DC cohort starting the following month, I knew it was an area I was meant to pursue and explore.

So, what really is it? According to Martin Seligman (2002), "positive psychology is the scientific study of optimal human functioning. It aims to discover and promote the factors that allow individuals and communities to thrive". Not just live, not just function, but THRIVE.

That wasn't exactly the definition I was expecting. I guess, like most people, I assumed positive psychology was some type of "happiology". I was more than pleasantly surprised when I learned that it wasn't. Instead, positive psychology enhances our well-being, by encouraging us and giving us the permission to be human- to experience the full range of human experiences and emotions. Wherever we're at, whatever we're experiencing, positive psychology gives us the tools to work through those tough experiences, learn from them, and grow.

This first poetic chapter explores the definition and history of positive psychology, provides a brief description of the PERMA-V model and positive psychology interventions (PPIs), and lays the foundation for a deeper dive into these concepts in future chapters.

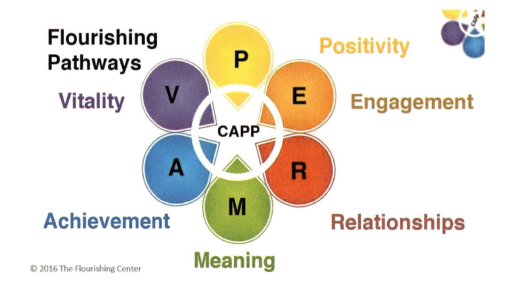

POSITIVE PSYCHOLOGY

Positive psychology
The science of human flourishing

A comprehensive wellness model
To get you north of neutral

Focusing on what's right with you
Not fixing all of your issues

Understanding perfection isn't necessary
Embracing the complexity of your humanity

Through self-awareness, self-compassion, and self-care
And the willingness to be present and be here

PERMA-V

I knew where I was at
I didn't want that

Just living wasn't enough for me
I wanted to be happy

And so I went searching
For that one thing to change everything

But not one thing was the answer
A lot of things matter, other people matter

Positivity
Engagement
Relationships

Meaning
Achievement
Vitality

These are the pathways to flourishing
CAPP's model- PERMA-V

HAPPINESS HISTORY

What does it mean to be happy
The question has a long history

At first happiness was survival
Something outside of our control

It's evolved into something attainable
Something inside of our control

Aristotle said happiness is a life of meaning
Epicurus said happiness is having positive experiences and feelings

Still others have mentioned
Aspiring towards Godlike perfection

Is happiness a self-evident truth
Is it a birthright to pursue

The idea of happiness has changed over time
But it's subjective, so yours to define

Yes, although happiness has a history
You have the freedom to write your own happiness story

THE HAPPINESS FORMULA

What contributes to my happiness
Is it biological or a result of life conditions

The answer is both and more
Voluntary activities also matter

If my biological set point is low
There is a way to make it grow

I am not destined to be forever unhappy
I can change my set point with intentional activity

Major life events don't have a strong influence
But changing habits and small positive actions make a difference

Taking consistent control of my thoughts, feelings and actions
Makes happiness set point change happen

POSITIVE INTERVENTIONS

What are positive psychology interventions (PPIs)

PPIs are the things you can do
To achieve a happier you

There are at least 12 to consider
And I will list them now, here

Expressing Gratitude
Cultivating Optimism
Avoiding Overthinking and Social Comparison
Practicing Acts of Kindness
Nurturing Social Relationships
Developing Strategies for Coping
Learning to Forgive
Increasing Flow Experiences
Savoring Life's Joys
Committing to Your Goals
Practicing Religion and Spirituality
Taking Care of your Body

PPIs take active, consistent practice
And can become your happiness habits

PPIs are simple and easy to incorporate
When you choose interventions that are a natural fit

The person-activity fit diagnostic tool
Helps you find the strategies that work for you

WHY you engage in certain activities or situations
Can shed significant light on your motivations

If you act to avoid feeling guilty or anxious
Your participation in the activity is forced

If you act because someone else wants you to
You aren't doing something YOU really want to do

However, if an activity feels natural to you
It is something you will want to do

If an activity is something you enjoy
You will want to do it more

If you value the activity
You will do it freely

The last three reasons describe intrinsic motivation
Choose activities that fit these and you will sustain them

CHAPTER 2
THE COMPLEX BRAIN

Our brains are complex. They are capable of storing and processing a tremendous amount of information, memories, and experiences. They help us make sense of the world around us and keep us safe from harm.

Our brains have the best intentions. BUT…because they default to the negative and primarily focus on identifying threats, we sometimes need to rewire them to see things more holistically. What we think, how we think, and how we respond to situations and environmental cues are not fixed. We can change our brains with attention, intention, and practice.

This concept was truly life-changing for me. I didn't understand why my thoughts would, more often than not, go negative first. I didn't like when I would get stuck in my negative thoughts and feel down longer than what I would have liked or felt was an appropriate response. I didn't know that there was absolutely nothing wrong with me and that my brain was really trying to help and protect me from harm. And… I was incredibly relieved, excited, and felt empowered to find that there was something (many things actually) I could do to manage those experiences and change my happiness set point.

This second chapter focuses on key brain topics such as mindset, mind chatter, perspective, thinking traps, and negativity bias.

THREE BRAINS

I have 3 brains
Inside my head
Each special and unique
With functions discreet

The lizard brain is primal
Concerned mostly with basic survival
It makes my body work subconsciously
It's how I breathe, taste, smell and see

The mammal brain protects me
Its main focus is security
It helps me identify what's threatening
And tells me to fight, freeze, or flee

The human brain is more complex
It features the neo-cortex
In charge of symbolic reasoning-
Language, abstraction, perception, and planning

All three brains are important
All equally significant
All interacting together
To help me function and be happier

think POSITIVE

NEGATIVITY BIAS

My brain is bias towards the negative
Thoughts of shame and worry fill my head
These thoughts are set as my default
I must find a way to stop their assault

A single negative thought is stronger
And carries a lot more weight
Than a single thought that is positive
But it doesn't have to be this way

Although negative is my initial reaction
To all things that happen
With deliberate practice and intention
I can create a new, more positive connection

Then eventually the scales will tip
Because of this more positive relationship
Between my head and the world around me
And I will be set free from negativity and be happy

THINKING TRAPS

Thinking traps
Are not rooted in fact
They keep you stuck in a belief
Imprisoned, not free

This being stuck
Is your monkey brain run amuck
You're fast forward on emotion
Without pausing for evaluation

Thinking traps become habits
Inflexible and inaccurate
You must recognize their presence
To accomplish transcendence

There are 7 you must learn
In order to turn
Away from the iceberg you see
And what's deeper underneath

Jumping to conclusions
Is the first
Ready, fire, aim
Without supporting evidence to claim

Second is overgeneralizing
That's when you're over-emphasizing
Performing a character assassination
Based on a single situation

Third is tunnel vision
You're on a hijacked mission
Letting yourself bleed out
From a single incision

Fourth is magnifying and minimizing
Evaluating unrealistically
The positive and negative you see
Giving errors more credibility

Fifth is personalization
Always and forever thinking
Me, me, me
It's all you can see

Next is externalization
Opposite of personalization
You, you, you
The fault of others, many or few

The final trap is mind reading
Who do you think you are?
Houdini?
Well that's just crazy

MINDSET

I have a fixed mindset
A limiting belief
Of myself…and my abilities
And this is damaging

I like what I'm naturally good at
And avoid challenges out of fear
That I'll fail or that you'll laugh at me
For being stupid or inferior

I've learned that I can change my mindset
And this gives me great hope
That with hard work and intention
My fixed mindset will become one of growth

So please help me make this change
With interventions, tried and true
You can start by not just praising me
But instead focusing on what I do

You'll never understand the gratitude
I'll feel for what you've done
You'll put me on a path to happiness
You'll show me that I've won

PROPHESY

Self-fulfilling prophecy

A thought that becomes a belief
And a belief that becomes true
Repeated and re-emphasized
As a result of what you do

"I am so stupid" she says
Because she flunked her test
But the truth is she didn't study
So she couldn't do her best

Her belief made her resistant
To homework and tutoring
She didn't learn the basic skills
And this kept her from flourishing

She still believes she's stupid
And continues to find evidence to support
She's a self-fulfilling prophecy
And a victim of distort

PLEASE DON'T PRAISE ME

Please don't praise me
I know you have the best intent
But hearing that I'm oh so great
Causes me worry and distress
What if I falter next time
Will you think of me as less
I feel good when you praise me
But it is fleeting and intense
I anxiously wait until the next time
When you can validate my worth again

I would rather that you tell me
What you liked about what I did
It puts the focus on the process, not me
And feels supportive rather than judging
You'll help me build self-confidence and self-efficacy
Which is more enduring than self-esteem
I'll be on the journey towards authentic happiness
And on the path to flourishing

Worry less live more

WORRY

Worry is irrational
Thoughts not normal
A negative fantasy
Not rooted in reality

It can lead to catastrophizing
A small event becomes devastating
A chain of worry with a seemingly linear relationship
But with no real, logical fit

Worry and anxiety
Wreak havoc on you body
They increase your hear rate
When asleep and awake

Stressors trigger worry
Be aware of thoughts stirring
Feel your emotions that simmer
But don't let them linger

The presence of worry
Is not overly concerning
But an extended length of stay
Can be cause for dismay

So take measures to limit
The time spent in it
Recognize it for its lesson
Scrutinize your answer to the "what's next" question

Worry alerts us
To a need to problem solve
Leading to resolve
Helping us further evolve

TALKING BACK TO MIND CHATTER

All this negative mind chatter
Running through my head
I want positive thoughts instead
There is a way ahead

To make this change
I must talk back or rearrange
Those thoughts holding me back
Conducting their vicious attack

But first I must notice them
Must be aware and must listen
Must acknowledge their pessimism
Must recognize their functionality and origination

Must see some error in their composition
Convince myself of a better vision
A better and more useful way of thinking
About life, myself, and why something may be happening

Talking back comes in many forms
Explaining why a thought is untrue
Providing an alternative point of view
Suggesting a more realistic future avenue

Talking back can change my chatter
Help me focus on the truth and what matters
With conscious and deliberate practice
I will know positivity and happiness

PERSPECTIVE

Put it in perspective
It's really not that bad
It's silly to catastrophize
And make yourself anxious and sad

It doesn't have to be like this
There are some proven tools
To help you focus on what's realistic
And make you feel more soothed

First think about the worst case
And then think about the best
The likely is somewhere in-between
The despair and the jest

It takes a little practice
And a little conscious thought
To change the default negative
And gain the peace you've sought

So next time you are feeling tense
Remember and please use
The PIP process described above
To chase away your blues

PROBLEM

What is the problem
Is it really me
Or is there something else
To explain the mess I see

Is the problem that I've identified
Accurate and true
Or should I get another opinion
To explore a different view

I know that just one story
Is limited and wrought
With my bias based on experiences
And learned ideas that I've been taught

I really want to solve this problem
That's why it's critical
To identify it correctly
By using this simple problem solving tool

First I write down what I think
And then I ask a friend
To help me generate more options
To debate and comprehend

The real problem will emerge
From this collaborative task
Now I'll be able to develop a real solution
And I'll be so happy that I'd asked

Your life doesn't get better by chance but by change

REALITY

Your thoughts create your reality
What you think about you will see
Who you believe you are you will be
It's a self-fulfilling prophesy

Thoughts are powerful and key
To creating the life you want, your destiny
So set your negative thoughts and worries free
And instead imagine yourself blissfully happy

BRAIN CHANGE

You can change your mind if you want
With consistent, deliberate, practiced thought
Focusing on what and who you want to be
Letting go of what you don't want and negativity

Creating new connections in your brain
Is the beginning of change
Repetitive practice will make them thick
It will also make the good thoughts stick

Your life will have a new trajectory
One that leads you to happy
Be patient for the change
Your thoughts need time to rearrange

You will have a stronger defense
To combat the ANTS you're fighting against
You will start to smile more and dance
And you will be so glad you took this chance

- ANTS = automatic negative thoughts

Chapter 3
POSITIVITY

The "P" in the PERMA-V model represents POSITIVITY. Positivity is NOT being positive all the time (can you imagine how exhausting that would be, plus it's unnatural) or having your head stuck in the clouds or buried in the ground, unable to see reality. I used to think being positive was both of those things, and then I learned that having that viewpoint set me up for disappointment, kept me trapped inside a very neat, perfect box, and forced me to into hiding when I wasn't feeling "happy" or "good".

Rather, positivity is more about having perspective, and being able to see the silver lining. It's easy to feel happy when things are going well, but it requires self-awareness, commitment, and mental agility to hunt and find the good stuff when faced with a challenging or uncomfortable life experience. But isn't that when we need positivity most? Well, yes and no. Consistently practicing positivity tools (in both good times and bad) creates more positive emotion… which can raise our biological set point thereby increasing our capacity for happiness, strengthening our positivity muscles, and giving us a fighting chance when adversity strikes.

Below are some simple definitions and key words to keep in mind while reading this chapter.

Positivity: "experiencing positive emotions such as happiness, satisfaction, self-regard, serenity, and cheerfulness on a regular basis."

Short definition: "optimism, happiness, and life-satisfaction"

"Mind is a flexible mirror, adjust it, to see a better world."- Amit Ray

Someone with a positive perspective:
Sees the glass as half full
Appreciates what he/she has
Recognizes the lesson in the struggle
Has hope for the future

Key poetic topics include: gratitude, savoring, kindness, resilience

GRATITUDE

Expressing Gratitude
Improves your mood
Demonstrates a positive attitude
Is oh so good for you

Practicing gratitude results in
Less negative self-preoccupation
More optimism
More life satisfaction

It increases positivity
Decreases stress and anxiety
Enables savoring
Makes you a better "me"

Focusing on 3 to 5 good things a day
No matter how exciting or mundane
Is a sure-fire way
To make you happier today

Or expressing your gratitude
To someone for something they do
Cultivates genuine appreciation
And develops more positive relations

SAVORING

When you savor
You capture the flavor
Of a person or activity
That makes you happy

You focus on a fond memory
Replay and re-feel the positivity
Which relieves current stress
And builds resilience

Savoring must be done
With focused attention and emotion
It is anchored in appreciation
Of the beauty in the things and people you love

Focus determines Reality

OPTIMISM

I'm on a mission
To create more optimism

To look at life a little differently
To look at life more positively

To see the glass as half full
Instead of empty without value

The lens through which I view it
Affects the way that I intuit

When I see life as opportunity
It fosters positive thinking

It reduces stress and conflict
What great benefits

My life view
Is something that I choose

I choose to look at life with more optimism
And experience more positive emotion

KINDNESS

Acts of kindness
Build personal happiness

They make me less self-centered
And more focused on others

But tend to benefit me as the giver
Even more than the receiver

Displaying generosity
Is evidence of a benevolent "me"

Being kind makes me feel good
Relieves me from the bondage of "should"

It creates an upwards spiral
Of positive feelings and goodwill

Being kind is good for me
Because it produces prosocial reciprocity

·CALLIGRAPHY·

PERMISSION TO BE HUMAN

I give myself the permission to be human

Permission to be an imperfect person
Permission to make mistakes
Permission to be wrong
Permission to fail

But I also give myself the permission to be awesome
Permission to follow my dreams
Permission to persevere and try again
Permission to be successful
…and the permission to be proud of that

Giving myself these permissions
Allows me to live a full, balanced life
To be present in the moment
Allows me to feel the full range of emotions
Allows me to experience gratitude

By giving myself the permission to be human, I give myself the permission and the pathway to happiness

·CALLIGRAPHY·

PENCIL

When you're feeling kind of down
And your face can't help but frown
Put a pencil in your mouth

When you're feeling kind of angry
And your face feels tight and clenchy
Put a pencil in your mouth

When you feel like you can't smile
And it's been quite a awhile
Put a pencil in your mouth

Just try it out and see
The changes in your body
Will make you feel happy

OPTIMISTIC THOUGHTS

The lens through which we see the world
Affects how we both think and feel
We can be a pessimist or optimist
It is a choice of thinking, not a trait

Our thoughts and minds are powerful
Learning to control them is an important tool
It takes practice in noticing and presence
And the willingness to challenge deference

We must identify the mind clutter
Understand our own explanatory model
Practice the ABCs of CBT
To change our habit of thinking

Our thoughts can be organized into clusters
Factual, fantasy, future, and judgmental
These types of thoughts have consequence
On things emotional, physical and mental

Our explanatory style
Helps us explain the why
There are 3 Ps which govern this
Personalization, permanence, and pervasiveness

Optimists and Pessimists explain things differently
One way is not better than the other necessarily
The problem is when you only have one way
When you are inflexible and unable to see the grey

And so we must learn CBT
On our own or in therapy
So that we can practice what we learn
And gain more optimistic thinking in turn

- ABC= activating event, belief, consequence
- CBT= cognitive behavioral therapy

RESILIENCE

What is resilience
Is it inheritable or learned
What can I do to get through those times
I've felt the struggle and have been burned

What is it that I must have within
In order to bounce back
To see the glass half full instead
To develop the mental toughness that I lack

There are factors of resilience
I must learn and put to practice
In order to "struggle well"
To bend not break, stay active

I must know and understand my emotions
Control them and my actions when I can
Have confidence that I can master this
And ask for help and support when I can't

I must make an effort to empathize
To read the cues people give but try to hide
To believe things will get better
To understand other, alternate sides

This will all take time and conscious effort
But I will work hard and do my best
And when I'm able to do all this
I will be happy and resilient

MORE SAVORING

When you savor…

Your thoughts are flavored
With memories you hold dear
With the present moment, now and here
With your hopes and dreams for the future

Reminiscence
Attentiveness
And Anticipation
Bring feelings of elation

You learn to marvel at life
Express gratitude, amidst strife
Bask in the glory of the day
Relax and luxuriate

…Take time to savor

CHAPTER 4
ENGAGEMENT

The "E" in the PERMA-V model represents ENGAGEMENT. Engagement is NOT just activity. Engagement is about connection to our life experiences. What activities make you smile? Who do you find yourself wanting to be around and spend time with? When are you so engrossed with what you're doing in this life that you lose track of time and seem to have boundless energy?

The answers to the above questions describe your flow experiences and engagement tools help you create more of them. Is it possible to always be in flow? Nope, that's not realistic. Are there non-flow activities we have to perform on a regular basis? Absolutely. It's difficult to be in flow (for me anyways) when I'm stuck in a traffic jam on I-95. The point here isn't to be in constant flow, it's to recognize what puts you in flow and consciously seek out, choose, and make time for those people and activities to show up in your life on a more regular basis.

Below are some simple definitions and key words to keep in mind while reading this chapter.

Engagement: "having interests and pursuits that deeply captivate us, resulting in the regular experience of flow and personal growth"

Short definition: "crafting more flow experiences"

"When we strike a balance between the challenge of an activity and our skill at performing it, when the rhythm of the work itself feels in sync with our pulse, when we know that what we're doing matters, we can get totally absorbed in our task. That is happiness."- Ariel Gore

Someone who is engaged with life:
Has a strong sense of self-awareness
Lives in the present moment
Participates in activities he/she loves
Consciously strives to make the world a better place

Key poetic topics include: engagement, flow, authenticity

ENGAGEMENT

When I'm engaged
I feel so amazed

In a space of flow
I'm in the zone

That challenging task
Keeps me proactive

To further develop my skills
And retain this feeling

To stay in this absorbed state
I must self-regulate

Eliminate distractions
For continuous, motivated action

Monitor and track
My progress and feedback

And with this prowess
I will manifest success

FLOW

Being in the flow

It feels so natural
I lose track of time
I feel sublime
This is what I'm meant for

I've waited for this feeling
For a very, very long while
And as I felt its impending approach
I couldn't stop my Duchene smile

I found meaning and purpose
In such a simple thing
Sharing tools proven to promote
Happiness, well-being, and flourishing

How did I get here
Was I always called to this
Or did my life experiences
Send me on this quest

I wasn't always happy
The opposite is true
But now that I've found this path
I give it graciously to you

EXTERNALS

You can be alone
But not feel lonely

Be with others
But not feel connected

Be successful at work
But not feel fulfilled

Be busy
But still feel bored

Smile on the outside
But not feel happy inside

The seemingly glorious externals
Do not predict feelings internal

It's sometimes easier to hide
Then to be open and confide

But this all comes at a cost
And produces feelings of loss

So instead of living on a stage
Live authentically and engaged

Be fearlessly authentic

AUTHENTICITY

Authenticity
Has no relativity

Be who you are
And you will go far

Make this a priority
And you will be happy

Live and speak your truth
Is what you must do

No need to confess
No unnecessary stress

No acting unreal
No hiding how you feel

You can relax in your skin
Embrace truly living

Your relationships will grow
With the people that know

Trust will deepen
In time and season

And real love can blossom
From living your awesome

TYRANNY OF CHOICE

The tyranny of choice
Is worthy of consider

Is more necessarily better
Is better necessarily bigger

Does all of this variety
Cause me stress and anxiety

Am I happy with "good enough"
Or is no choice ever "good enough"

Am I prone to the constant re-consider
That leaves me feeling choice-bitter

When I choose do I feel free
Or does choice imprison me

Do I have time to evaluate
Enough time to deliberate

Can my brain handle the choice volume
Or is it deaf to all the options

In my answers to these questions
Lies important lessons

About how I should approach life decisions
With intellect or intuition

It takes delicate balance
To perform this decision dance

CHAPTER 5
RELATIONSHIPS

The "R" in the PERMA-V model represents RELATIONSHIPS. There are many types of relationships when you define a relationship as "the way in which two or more people talk to, behave toward, and deal with each other"(Merriam-Webster). Our focus here, however, is on meaningful relationships.

How do we create more meaningful relationships? How do we enhance the meaningful relationships that already exist? How do we nurture a relationship that is suffering?

Communication plays an integral role. But not just any type of communication…the words we use matter, our non-verbal cues (presence) set a tone, and the degree of vulnerability, compassion, and forgiveness we have with both ourselves and others impact the strength of our connections.

When asked to describe positive psychology, Dr. Chris Peterson simply said: "other people matter". Make the choice, take the time, and do the work to develop, enhance, and sustain meaningful connections in your life.

Below are some simple definitions and key words to keep in mind while reading this chapter.

Relationships: "experiencing affection, friendship, and love (in both directions) with other (human) beings in different contexts (family, leisure, work)."

Short definition: "authentic, meaningful, life-enhancing connections"

"We have to recognize that there cannot be relationships unless there is commitment, unless there is loyalty, unless there is love, patience, persistence." -Cornel West

Someone who has strong relationships:
Has a reliable community of friends he/she can be vulnerable with
Has learned the art of being a good listener
Nurtures the good connection he/she has with others
Knows when it is necessary to let go of a relationship

Key poetic topics include: forgiveness, presence, trust, vulnerability, love languages

SOCIAL RELATIONSHIPS

There's you
There's me
There's we

Building the we between us
Means proactively enhancing the quality of our relationship

Going deeper with each other
Really being present and there

Strengthening the existing connection
From an acquaintanceship to an authentic friendship

This requires time and effort
But the benefits are worth the work

Prosocial reciprocity
Mutual experiences of efficacy

A happier you
A happier me
A happier we

Let it Go

FORGIVENESS

I forgive you
I forgive me
Because forgiveness is key
To living happy

I forgive us
For our wrongs
For the hurts we've caused
For foolishly acting without pause

I do this freely
Without vengeance
Without resentment
Without thoughts of revenge

I let go of those negative feelings
In order to grow in character
In order to feel happier
In order to feel healthier

Forgiveness is a gift
A gift that is free
A gift I give to me
The gift of serenity

MORE ON FORGIVENESS

Without forgiveness
Life can feel like a mess

But the act of forgiving
Is a real blessing

It is something I do for me
To set myself free

It is a gift I give to you
So that our relationship stays true

It allows me to let go
It allows me to grow

It helps me find relief
It helps me find peace

Yes, forgiveness fills my hole
Forgiveness feeds my soul

It can be difficult to practice
But its rewards are everlasting

PRESENCE

Being present
Is the best present
Being fully aware
Shows people you care

It demonstrates interest
It's giving others your best
It's a mark of appreciation
And worthy of repetition

You are able to genuinely connect
To be honest and direct
Really listen and reflect
Be a better friend

Being present is a gift
A gift whose cost is free
A gift when freely given
Is the precious gift of me

RELATIONSHIPS

A relationship is meant to be
A source of joy
And a source of ecstasy
Shared between you and me

It takes vulnerability
It requires integrity
It's grounded in honesty
It blooms with authenticity

Characterized by trust and empathy
Marked with sincerity
Yields a sense of safety
And feelings of security

These are the qualities
We can achieve
With a relationship
Of flourishing

NEGATIVE AFFECT

Negative affect
Can have serious effects

It can impair our physical system
Can result in prolonged depression and inflammation
Can lead to heart attack
Who wants that

It's commonly described
As feeling bad or sad
But those feelings aren't necessarily a problem
Unless you get stuck in them

There are things you can do to influence
Your negative affect experience
Satisfying relationships make a difference
Ground yourself in authentic, reliable friendships

UPSIDE

The upside
Of the dark side
Comes with letting
Someone inside

To help you release the pain
Release the hate
Release the bad
Release the sad

To help you gain acceptance
Gain perspective
Gain a sense of peace
Gain happiness

To help you change your attitude
To one of gratitude
And feelings of loneliness
Into feelings of abundance

To help you recognize the necessity
Of displaying vulnerability
And of living with authenticity
To overcome the negativity

Good things take Time

TRUST

For there to be trust
Then there must

Be credibility
Be reliability
Be intimacy
Be a healthy orientation towards me

These qualities take time
To develop and grow
To be authentically our own
To become to others, known

Trust is essential and key
For two people to be
Together yet free
And truly happy

VULNERABILITY

Vulnerability
Can be quite scary
Yes, letting myself be seen
Can feel unnerving

What will you think
What will you say
Will you be accepting
Or will you walk away

Can I trust you with my secrets
Can I trust you with my heart
Can I trust you to support me when things are good
But more importantly can I trust you when I'm falling apart

Will you really listen to me speak my truth
Will you show me compassion and care
Will you assure me that I still belong
Will you continue urging me to share

If you still think of me lovingly
If you still stand by my side
If your answers to my questions are yes
Then our relationship will flourish

APPRECIATION

By showing appreciation
We are establishing connection
We are demonstrating gratitude
A positive emotion and intervention

We are creating pathways to savoring
And doing so intentionally
Allowing ourselves and others
To extend our experiences of happy

When I tell you something I'm excited about
Please support me and be excited too
Show interest and ask me more about it
I'll be delighted when you do

I'll authentically reciprocate
When you share wins with me
Our relationship will deepen
And so will our intimacy

SOCIAL CONNECTION

Social connection
Is integral to life
Without it we feel lonely
Without it life is tough

Who we connect and network with
Is an important choice
We tend to subconsciously mimic them
In behavior, emotion, and voice

It's said 3 degrees of separation
Is all it really takes
To significantly influence or alter
Someone else's fate

We are here to support each other
We are here to be in relationship
We were never meant to be alone
We were always meant to flourish

LOVE LANGUAGE

If you love me
Then please show me
Show me in a way that I can receive
Show me in a way performed authentically
Show me in a way that is meaningful to me

Let me help you know what to do
By sharing my love languages with you
These are ways that I prefer to give and receive love
And by understanding the best ways to love communicate
We can better heart relate

I feel your love most fully with touch
And when you tell me how much
You see my transcendent beauty
You appreciate my depth and honesty
And deeply care for me

I also want to know
The best ways for me to show
The gratitude and love I feel for you
In the ways you feel are most true
Yes, please share and I will do

This is incredibly important to me
I want us to know and see
How much we both truly mean
To one another daily
This will build our intimacy

PASSION

Passion
Is a love condition
It brings people together
But doesn't always last forever
It's inspired by attraction
But subject to hedonistic adaptation

Maintaining passion in a relationship
Takes commitment and work
Both people must put forth effort
To stay desirable and connected
The attraction is not limited to physical
It is also emotional and cerebral

Alone passion is not enough
Lasting love needs other stuff
Compassion and commitment
Fun and enjoyment
Communication and understanding
Trust and vulnerability

CHAPTER 6
MEANING

The "M" in the PERMA-V model represents MEANING and PURPOSE. Why are we here? What is the purpose of this life? What is my role in it all? These are pretty hefty questions when you are expecting the answers to be at the level of some grand scale achievement or impact award or to be permanent in nature. Yes, the answers can be such, but consider what would happen if we expanded our minds about this concept.

Meaning and purpose can be found in religion or spirituality, in the raising of a family, in the work that you do, in volunteer activities, in the sharing of the special talent you've been given to a person, small group, community, or to the world at large. Yes, your meaning and purpose is unique to you. Social comparison here robs you of joy. Never underestimate the ripple effects that can happen when you live your purpose. And guess what…your purpose can change over time as your life changes and as you grow and evolve as a person.

Below are some simple definitions and key words to keep in mind as your reading this chaper.

Meaning and Purpose: "believing in and working towards something that transcends ourselves and our lifetimes, be it in the secular or spiritual domain."

Short definition: "creating purpose, passion, and fulfillment"

"The meaning of life is to find your gift. The purpose in life is to give it away."- Pablo Picasso

Someone who has a strong sense of meaning/purpose:
Believes there is a "why" to his/her life
Uses his/her unique gifts to make the world a better place
Lives his/her life with intention and with conscious thought and action
Understands that we're all connected and there IS a larger purpose to life

Key poetic topics include: purpose, meaning, spirituality

find your passion

PURPOSE AND MEANING

Purpose and meaning
Are not the same thing

But they are related
And strongly correlated

Meaning is a subjective feeling
Purpose is a knowing

Meaning spurs comprehension
Purpose fuels action

Meaning positively correlates with post traumatic growth
Purpose positively correlates with life satisfaction and hope

Having meaning leads to resiliency
Having purpose leads to flourishing

LIFE'S PURPOSE

What is life's purpose
Is it happiness

Or is life's purpose about serving
And bringing utility

Life's purpose can be either
Or it can be both or neither

Your life's purpose is individual
And something only you can know

It is how you uniquely impact the world
By the life that you build

Finding purpose is a journey
One of continuous searching

It's based on the things that you value
And the passions stirring within you

The skills that you develop along the way
The collection of life experiences you gather every day

Knowing your purpose generates positive feelings
It also expands longevity

Knowing your purpose makes you more psychologically healthy
It also helps reduce anxiety

Purpose is a verb
Sourced in spirituality, volunteering, and work

Pre-supposed by curiosity
And a sense of positivity

Find your purpose and you will be
On your own path to happy

MY GIFT

I give the world my gift
The gift that is authentically me
The gift of both giving and being
The person I was meant to be

It took me awhile to know
I needed time to experience and grow
Time to discover my passion
Time to put my passion into action

Action inspired by my unique interests
Action that utilizes my talents
Action that never feels like work
Because it just fits

This gift I give the world
The gift that is authentically me
I give it happily and freely
It is my reason for being here, my legacy

SPIRITUALITY

Spirituality is a feeling felt inside of me
Of deep intimacy
To something greater than me
To all that surrounds me

It provides me purpose and meaning
Gives me a sense of belonging
Infuses me with energy
Increases my calm and positivity

It helps me answer the tough questions
Who am I
What is my life for
Who is the creator

Spirituality is sacred practice
I can make part of everyday
When I take time to pray
And consciously live my faith

CHAPTER 7
ACHIEVEMENT

The "A" in the PERMA-V model represents ACHIEVEMENT. This includes both the small and large successes in life. Again, no need for social comparison here. What might be considered a "great achievement" may have cost someone something else of greater value. It's more about what is personally fulfilling for YOU.

Reaching a goal feels good. It builds our confidence, self-esteem, and self-efficacy. It also motivates us to do and be more. But, the kinds of goals we set also matter.

The goals we set should be both realistic and challenging. It's easy to stay in our comfort zones, but outside of the comfort zone is where real growth happens. This is where outside support and encouragement are helpful. I know, personally, that I sometimes need to be pushed to stretch my comfort zone. That can be uncomfortable at times, but definitely worth it.

Below are some simple definitions and key words to keep in mind while reading this chapter.

Achievement: "experiencing a sense of accomplishment (being a success story) on a regular basis, be it in the occupational domain or in our private lives"

Short definition: "accomplishment, inspired action"

"If you don't go after what you want, you'll never have it. If you don't ask, the answer is always no. If you don't step forward, you're always in the same." – Nora Roberts

Someone high in achievement:
Looks for and savors the successes in life- large and small
Sets goals, commits to them, and achieves them
Strives for continuous improvement
Supports and celebrates the achievement of others

Key poetic topics include: goals, visualization, achievement, talent, luck, self-efficacy

GOALS

A good goal is personal and meaningful

It's specific and challenging
Something worthy of pursuing
Reaching it requires significant effort
Commitment, self-regulation and self-management

Being intrinsically motivated to achieve it
Will help you maintain continuous effort
Be more willing to commit
Making you more likely to achieve it

Achievement builds self-esteem
Makes you proud of "me"
Increases satisfaction and productivity
Helps build self-efficacy

Goal setting and goal reaching makes you happy

GOAL SETTING

Setting and achieving goals
Feels wonderful
Goals give life meaning and purpose
And are indicative of growth and progress

In order to set goals
There are a few things you must know
Know what you want and what not doing you'll regret
Know your intent

Goal setting theory
Is a framework for goal setting deliberately
The steps are: set, develop, plan, act
Monitor, evaluate, and celebrate success

The best goals are SMART+
Specific, measurable, and achievable to start
Realistic, timely and simplified to chart
Challenging enough to maintain motivational spark

Setting cues known as primers
Give you regular reminders
Of the goals you can achieve
With sustained action and belief

VISUALIZATION

Visualization
Stirs the imagination
Is a form of mental stimulation

It can help you get what you desire
Help you be what you aspire
Help you perform in ways that inspire

Visualization can be accomplished through fantasizing
Achieved through dramatizing
Or depicted on a vision board synthesizing

Visualization is not limited to visual
It can be the re-creation of a feeling or smell
All of these forms work well

Visualization can focus on the outcome or process
Process visualization is usually the best
Put both to the test

You will be surprised by the manifestation
Elated by your own creation
Of the life or outcome you've been long awaiting

ACHIEVEMENT

In order to achieve
You must believe
You must have hope
To reach your goals

You must have motivation
To put your plans into action
You must measure your progress
And continuously assess

You must have patience
Because achievement is a timely process
Achieving goals takes changes
And changes happen in stages

In stage 1, precontemplation
You are unaware of the situation
You don't recognize the need
And so you concede

In stage 2, contemplation
You recognize the need for innovation
You see the issues clearly
You see possibilities

In stage 3, planning
You are actively developing
Your action plan and timeline
And other necessary guidelines

In stage 4, action
You are making things happen
Your intentional behaviors
Are making progress to savor

In stage 5, maintenance
You are working towards permanence
You are monitoring continued action
To see if lasting change can happen

In stage 6, relapse/termination
You are deciding on future action
Do you need to relapse and adapt
Or have you reached success

THE TALENT MYTH

I'm really not good at that
I don't have the raw talent
These are the feelings of lament
Which accompany a fixed mindset

Talent is a myth I heard
And the thought I can't learn- absurd
I must believe I can improve
Through hard work, practice, and attitude

Little by little it happens
With consistent effort over time
The thing I never thought I could do
Becomes a strength skill of mine

It may take years to cultivate
At least 10 years to bloom full
But with deliberate practice and momentum
I can become exceptional

THE LUCK FACTOR

I feel so lucky
For all the good that has happened to me
I never understood why I've been so blessed
But now I know it's because I've lived with zest

I've approached my life with an open mind
Paid attention to opportunities as they unwind
Based my decisions on intuition
Created self-fulfilling prophesies from positive expectations

When I've come to a potential roadblock
I've focused on the possibility, not the stop
Have been resilient because of reframing
Have turned bad luck into good, unending

You can have this luck too
By following the principles I've just shared with you
You can change your luck and your life's show
Without a leprechaun, pot of gold, or rainbow

SELF-EFFICACY

It's all about me
Building self-esteem
Building self-efficacy
Feeling good about and believing in me

Self-efficacy is necessary
For relieving depression and anxiety
For reaching goals and problem solving
For resiliency and well being

Having role models and cheerleaders
Managing stress and mastery experiences
Savoring wins and knowing your worth
Is all building self-efficacy work

It is work worth doing
You are worth your own investing
With self-efficacy you can grow to be
That amazing person you are meant to be

Chapter 8
VITALITY

The "V" in the PERMA-V model represents VITALITY. Being mentally, physically, and spiritually fit and balanced increases the quality of our life experiences.

The mind-body connection has been highly under-valued in Western culture and we are just starting to understand it and practice it. The food we eat, the amount of sleep we get, the way we move, rest, and feel about our bodies, and our ability to practice mindfulness all impact our energy levels and our capacity to metabolize and digest our life experiences.

Below are some simple definitions and key terms to keep in mind as you read this chapter.

Vitality: "taking good care of our bodies and minds, for example via regular physical exercise, a healthy diet, enough sleep, and mindfulness practice".

Short definition: "optimal wellness; strong, healthy bodies"

"Your health is what you make of it. Everything you do and think either adds to the vitality, energy and spirit you possess or takes away from it."- Ann Wigmore

A truly vital person:
Takes care of his/her body, mind, and spirit
Knows when to engage and when to relax
Manages his/her energy
Practices mindfulness

Key poetic topics include: exercise, sleep, rest, energy, mindfulness

MIND

BODY

SOUL

SPIRIT

TAKING CARE OF MIND AND BODY

Taking care of my mind and body
Is oh so good for me

It keeps me healthy
Increases my immunity

Reduces my stress and anxiety
Improves my vitality

Gives me more energy
Makes me happy

Taking care of my mind and body
Is oh so good for me

It requires purposeful intention
Continuous, motivated action

Being self-compassionate and self-aware
Enables self-care

I receive a needed mental and physical cleaning
By exercising and meditating daily

Yes, taking care of mind and body
Is oh so good for me

EGO REPLETION

My mental fuel
Is a limited pool

I must harness it
For optimal benefit

Manage my stress
Manage crisis

Manage my energy
Manage my activity

Take care of my body
Eat to not get hangry

Make time to exercise
And get re-energized

Get plenty of sleep
To not further deplete

Build my self-regulation muscle
To improve my self-control

All of these intentional acts
Will replete and improve my synapse

There will be enough mental gas in my brain
To thrive, conquer challenges, and sustain

MINDFULNESS

Are you being mindful
Or is your mind full

With things that don't matter
Or endless mind chatter

Are you concentrating on the present
Or focusing on past resentments

Do you pay attention to people
Or are you only concerned with your ego

Do you see reality
Or are you lost in fantasy

Ask yourself these questions
Know you can change with intention

Can learn to think and accept
With calm and without judgment

That you are not the center of the universe
But still incredibly meaningful and important

Mindfulness meditation is key
To conserving and managing your energy

Calm and quiet your mind
To relax and unwind

Put yourself in meditation space
Just five minutes a day

And you'll be on your way to living
Your best life, one of true vitality

let yourself rest

REST

Rest
Relax
Be still
Sleep

Rest your eyes
Rest your body
Rest your mind
Rest in peace

Relax your thoughts
Relax your breath
Relax control
Relax and unwind

Be still and listen
Be still in knowing
Be still in silence
Be still the night

Sleep to recharge
Sleep to renew
Sleep to dream subconsciously
Get your beauty sleep

For optimal benefit
To live in balance
To live your best life
Rest, relax, be still, sleep

SLEEP

Getting a good night's rest
Helps us feel our best

It allows our bodies to recharge
And our minds to discharge

How much sleep we get matters
It affects our sleep and dream patterns

Dreaming happens in REM
That's where it all begins

The unlocking of our subconscious
The window to our deepest thoughts

7 to 8 hours sleep a day
Is the suggested remedy

15 minute naps too
Can help us temporarily renew

So don't skimp on sleep
If you want to feel your most elite

EXERCISE

Exercise
To stay alive
To feel alive
To be alive

Move your body
In ways you love
In ways that are fun
In ways that challenge

Physical activity
Is good for your body
Is good for your mentality
Is good for your vitality

Make time in your day
To do some everyday
Make exercise part of your routine
To stay healthy, happy, and serene

9781504371384